THE SCULPTURED IMAGE

The Burghers of Calais, by Rodin. Detail of hand. *Roger-Viollet*

Franklin Watts, Inc., 575 Lexington Avenue, New York, N.Y. 10022

THE SCULPTURED IMAGE

The art of sculpture as seen in monuments to gods,
men, and ideas

Illustrated with photographs

by Lamont Moore

**Author of The First Book of Architecture and
The First Book of Paintings**

To Florence Bradley Moore
who could have been a sculptress, but
preferred to be the mother of the author,
this book is dedicated

Library of Congress Catalog Card Number: 67-17511
© Copyright 1967 by Lamont Moore
Printed in the United States of America
1   2   3   4   5

INTRODUCTION

What is an image? The word has several meanings. An image can be a vague phantom of the imagination or the reflection of a face in a mirror. An image is also the **visible representation** of something man sees in the world: a tree, a flower, a human being. Or it is the **visible representation** of something seen in the mind's eye—an invented form never before seen in the world.

Every artist is an image-maker. The painter creates images on flat surfaces; the sculptor fashions them in space. His images have the three dimensions of height, width, and depth, whether they are sculptured pictures on a wall or statues standing free so that we can walk around them to view them from all sides.

The sculptor usually creates his images from long-lasting materials such as stone or metal. They can stand outdoors for centuries. Sculpture is, therefore, the most practical art for monuments to gods, or memorials to famous people. It also can express dramatically universal ideas: Liberty, Freedom, Peace.

Where are these sculptured images? They are everywhere—in cities and towns and far from the habitations of man, on the tops of mountains or carved into cliffs. The purpose of this book is to visit by means of photographs some noted monuments that still remain where they were erected. We shall see only a few that have been removed to museums in order that they may be preserved. We shall look at some sculpture ages old and at some quite new, in order to become familiar with the entire span of sculptural history around the world.

We shall discover that sculptors use elements found in all works of art. Especially they use **line, shape** enclosed by line, and **form** to show the volume that the image occupies in **space.** The elements are arranged according to the principles of **pattern, balance, rhythm, contrast,** and **unity.**

When one realizes how much a sculptor must know about the materials he uses, as well as about the elements and principles required for every work of art, it is obvious that as an artist he must be a man of skill. It is not surprising to learn that the word "art" comes from a Latin word the ancient Romans used when they wanted to say "skill."

THE SCULPTURED IMAGE

The Image of Gods as Monsters

Sphinx. Giza, Egypt.

The Great Sphinx at Giza, Egypt, is one of the oldest and most famous monuments in the world. The head is that of King Chephren, who reigned about 2850 B. C. and whose tomb is in the pyramid to the right. For almost five thousand years this face has looked toward the rising sun. The king wears the headgear of ancient Egyptian rulers, consisting of a cap with two winglike coverings at the sides, ornamented on the forehead with the sacred snake, of which only a V-shaped wedge remains. The body is that of a lion, to suggest that Chephren was as brave and strong as the king of beasts.

Many years after the Sphinx was completed, another king found it almost covered by desert sand. Between its legs there is a tall stone tablet that tells of the task of removing the tons of sand so as to free this image of royal power.

There are not many man-beast images in the sculpture of the Western world. Therefore we are not as accustomed to them as are the people in India and China, where such sculptures abound. These half-human, half-animal forms were not intended to represent creatures that really lived. They appear to us as monsters, but we should consider them as symbols of ideas. The unknown sculptors who created the Sphinx were given the task of representing an image of eternal, godlike, and kingly power. This was achieved in various sculptural ways.

Since the pyramid was enormous, the monument also had

1

opp. page **The Sphinx.**

to be very large if it were not to be lost in the desert landscape. When planning a monument, a sculptor always considers the problem of size, or scale. Fortunately there was a large outcrop of rock near the pyramid. It was decided to transform that rock into one great reclining figure, a huge sculpture in the round. The Sphinx is complete on all sides and can be viewed from every angle.

While sculptors were shaping the rock with hammers and chisels they kept the forms of the various parts of the statue large and simple. Delicate shapes and fine lines would have been out of place on such a large mass. They carved the head set squarely on the shoulders and they made the legs of equal length, projecting toward us. The right side of the image is the same as the left in order to obtain "bisymmetric" balance, which always creates an impression of stability.

The Sphinx is grand and awesome even though it has been partially ruined by time. Its size and dignity befit the image of a king who was also a god according to the religious beliefs of the ancient Egyptians.

Assyrian Fertility God.

Before looking at the picture on page 3, reach into your pocket and take out a coin. Perhaps you never realized that when you buy something you pay for it with a piece of sculpture. The image on each side of a coin is relief sculpture, with forms projecting from a flat background. Reliefs may project only slightly, as in coins or medals, for which designs are usually modeled in clay. Or reliefs may project so that they are almost completely separated from their backgrounds, as

2

opp. page **Assyrian Eagle-headed Figure.** *Yale University Art Gallery*

in carved stone decorations for buildings. The word "sculptor" comes from a Latin word meaning "to carve."

Sculptors in ancient Assyria excelled at carving low reliefs depicting lion hunts and battles. These scenes decorated palaces and were interspersed with images of Assyrian gods, like the one from the palace of King Ashurnasirpal II, who reigned 884-859 B.C., now at the Yale University Art Gallery. The god is represented as an eagle with a man's body. He dusts pollen on the blossoms of a date-palm tree to ensure a good harvest of fruit. His "eagle eye," carved more deeply than any other part of the image, attracts our attention immediately.

He is also a kingly god wearing a fringed and tasseled robe. There is no doubt that he is powerful. The muscles on his arms and leg show great strength and are in contrast to the crisp, straight lines of the splendid wings. The fine details in this relief give texture to the surface. Notice that the sculptor did not cover the entire panel with carving. He smoothed broad, flat areas around the figure to set it off majestically.

Perhaps you are now beginning to appreciate the basic differences between the two kinds of sculpture. Sculpture in the round tends to emphasize form and space. Relief sculpture tends to stress line and pattern.

The Image of Gods as Men

Shiva Trimurti. Island of Elephanta, Bombay, India.

We have looked at two examples of the image of gods as monsters. Glancing at the picture on page 6, one might think that unknown sculptors of the eighth or ninth century A. D. had created the image of a human monster—a freak with three human heads. On the contrary, this is a symbolic sculpture of three aspects of one god merged into a single image, according to the Hindu religious beliefs. The word "murti" in the Hindu language means "image." Therefore, "trimurti" signifies the "three-image" of the god Shiva.

This gigantic sculpture, sixteen feet high, was carved in the wall of a cave hewn from solid rock, with supports of stone in the form of columns. Although badly damaged by vandals, the "Trimurti" is one of the great monuments of Indian art.

The awesome head in the center represents Shiva the Preserver, Lord of the Noonday Sun and the Sun at Midnight, when it was thought to be under the earth reposing on the serpent of eternity. Encircling his throat are a strand of pearls, representing the planets, and a golden collar set with the five jewels of the cosmic elements.

To the right is Shiva the Creator, Lord of the Rising Sun. Leaves and flowers decorate his headdress.

To the left is Shiva the Destroyer, Lord of the Setting Sun and Lord of Death, which is indicated by the skull carved above his left eye.

The towering crown of the central head was originally decorated with three disks to represent the suns of morning, noon, and evening.

Notice how the heads are connected by their headdresses, which flow one into the other as day flows into night, spring into summer, birth into death. The faces are quite separate, their forms rounded, almost soft, in appearance. But there is a sharpness in the outlines. The broad shoulders of Shiva the Preserver provide a firm base for the sculpture, suggesting that "the three aspects of the one" are eternal.

The Olympian Zeus.

The Greeks visualized their gods not as monsters, but as perfect human beings. Sculptors selected the most-admired proportions of human anatomy and combined them to achieve "ideal" figures and faces that few human beings possess. It took several centuries for the Greeks to develop images of their gods. About 460 B.C. the sculptor Phidias brought the art of Greek sculpture to a high degree of perfection with his "Olympian Zeus" and later with his world-famous architectural sculpture for the Parthenon in Athens.

Phidias constructed his "Zeus" in the temple at Olympia, site of the Olympic games. He used stone, wood, ivory, and precious metals to erect a seated figure of the "king of gods and men" that rose to the height of forty-five feet. For eight hundred years this colossus was one of the Seven Wonders of the Ancient World. Travelers came from afar to marvel at the naturalness of the image. When vandals and fire destroyed both the temple and the statue, only a few coins and the

opp. page   **Shiva Trimurti. Elephanta, India.**

London School of Oriental and African Studies

written accounts of visitors to the temple remained to tell us something about this masterpiece of Greek art.

Perhaps there is another echo of Phidias' sculpture in the magnificent head of Zeus, now in the Vatican Museum in Rome, pictured on page 9. It may have been carved by a pupil of Phidias. This is an "ideal" head, its features established by a standard of excellence determined by Phidias and other Greek sculptors. We are not accustomed to seeing the ideal in real life. Therefore the head of Zeus appears very grand, and remote from us—an appropriate image of a god in human form.

Coin of Elis, Greece.   *Berlin National Museum*

opp. page   **Zeus. Vatican Museum, Rome.**   *Alinari-Art Reference Bureau*

Christ. Amiens Cathedral, Amiens, France.

According to the New Testament section of the Christian Bible, God the Father came to earth in the person of Jesus Christ, who lived among men and taught that the spirit, or soul, in each man was eternal. There was danger that man could damage his soul by evil deeds, however. If, for example, he was cruel to his fellowmen, his soul after death could not join good souls in the City of God which is Heaven, but would descend instead into Hell.

It was not until about one thousand years after Christ's death that the Christian religion captured the imagination of most of the people of western Europe. Then they began to build great cathedrals with towers that pointed toward Heaven. By their beauty the cathedrals suggested that they were cities of God on earth. Light streamed into them through stained-glass windows. Sculptors decorated the doorways, walls, and even the lofty spires with marvelous sculptures that told the story of Christ.

At Amiens Cathedral, in France, the figure of Christ stands outside the central door. This statue (about A.D. 1225) is one of the most noted examples of sculpture in the world, as you may realize from the illustration. Christ raises one hand toward Heaven in the sign of blessing. He treads on two animals that represent the forces of evil. Notice how the noble head seems to shine forth from the shadow cast by the scalloped stone canopy. The face is smooth; the hair and beard are carved in a flowing manner. The upper garment is also smooth, thereby setting off the face. The folds of the cloak are massive by contrast and suggest the power of Christ, which is emphasized by the fullness and weight of the entire figure.

10

opp. page **Christ. Amiens Cathedral, France.** *Marburg-Art Reference Bureau*

God the Father. Breisach Cathedral Altarpiece, Breisach, Germany.

The stone sculpture we have just looked at and this image carved in wood provide an excellent comparison of the results that sculptors obtain by using different materials. Stone is a dense substance. It resists the sculptor's chisel. Stone is also rather brittle. If it is too finely carved, without some support left behind it, small pieces break away. Wood, on the other hand, is more yielding to the chisel. It is also self-supporting, and because of this it may be pierced and grooved and still remain in place.

The "Christ at Amiens" is massive, motionless, and majestic. "God the Father," at Breisach, Germany, made in the sixteenth century by the unknown sculptor with the initials H.L., is delicate, full of motion, and tragic. Magnificently crowned, God holds in His fleshy hand the scepter signifying power over the orb of this world. With furrowed brow, lined face, and searching eyes, He seems to be a sorrowing monarch, but an intensely human one who loves His people.

The image of Christ is "ideal" in the same way that the head of Zeus on page 9 is. This image of God the Father is personal, or natural. It could be the face of the sculptor's father, a specific man. Here sculpture has moved away from the impersonal, classic forms—perfect but remote, like the Greek gods—to romantic forms where the expression of individual human feelings is more important than the expression

13

opp. page   **God the Father. Breisach Cathedral, Germany.**   *Marburg-Art Reference Bureau* of pure, impersonal images. The great Italian sculptor Michelangelo helped to bring about this change.

Turn back to the "Christ at Amiens." Look at the picture with half-closed eyes. You will see that details disappear, but form remains. Look at "God the Father" in the same way. You will see that form disappears, but the sparkling play of light and shadow, made possible by the intricate wood carving, persists as an elaborate line pattern over the entire surface. This is especially noticeable in the serpent-like coils of the beard.

Michelangelo in his studio. From a painting by Cabanel.

THE IMAGE OF MEN AS GODS

Moses. San Pietro in Vincoli, Rome, Italy.

The picture on page 14 tells us much about Michelangelo, one of the most famous artists of all time. The architect-sculptor-painter rests for a moment in his studio. He holds his hammer and chisel, tools of the sculptor's trade. Like most artists of the Italian Renaissance, he was a man of many talents who excelled at whatever he attempted. Evidences of his genius are all around him.

Near his feet lie his architectural plans for the dome of St. Peter's Basilica, in Rome. On each side and behind him are three of the sculptured figures he carved for a Pope's tomb, as well as his renowned "Pieta," with the Virgin's head covered to protect it from dust. An unfinished painting of archangels sounding trumpets for the Last Judgment stands behind his desk, where he relaxed to write an occasional poem.

Unfortunately, because his abilities were so much in demand, Michelangelo was often forced to stop what he was doing and start something new. This meant that many of his projects, including the Pope's tomb, were left unfinished. So many interruptions sometimes angered the quick-tempered artist and sometimes plunged him into fits of melancholy, for he was both a violent and a gentle soul.

He was also a very hard worker. He insisted on using the finest marble, and spent long hours at the quarry supervising the stonecutters as they removed huge blocks from the mountain. Once the blocks were in his studio, he attacked them with his tools, to free the images he visualized within them.

15

Notice the position that Michelangelo has assumed as he gazes thoughtfully at his "Moses." His right shoulder, arm, and leg project forward. His left shoulder, arm, and leg recede. Now look at the pose of the completed statue on page 17.

Moses, the friend of God, is also seated, but his form is not relaxed. Unlike Michelangelo's position in his studio, the arm and right hand of Moses recede to shelter the Tablets of the Law, but his right leg projects. His left arm projects as his left leg recedes. These oppositions in the arrangement of the body, as well as its twisting, were intentionally created by Michelangelo to infuse his sculpture with powerful life and movement. The artist altered nature—the normal appearance of a seated person—to represent the image of Moses as a forceful man, almost a god, who warns, rewards, punishes, and leads. It seems as if Moses might suddenly stand up and turn his face toward us in anger or in love.

Other elements in this work reveal the sculptor's craft. He carved the muscles of the arms and legs unnaturally large to indicate strength. He balanced the heavy, flowing beard with the stiff folds of the robe that fill in the awkward space between the legs and create a massive, solid base for the statue.

Michelangelo was of the opinion that a well-made piece of sculpture could be rolled downhill and not be damaged. In other words, he favored compact, closed forms rather than open forms with many projections. We tend to see in all closed-form sculpture an enduring grandeur, eternal as a monument. We call such sculpture monumental, even if it is not created specifically to honor a person or a historical event.

16

Sculptors after Michelangelo imitated his twisting, violent, almost terrifying forms, but they forgot to follow his instruc-

opp. page   **Moses, by Michelangelo. San Pietro in Vincoli, Rome.**

Alinari-Art Reference Bureau

tions to keep these forms closed. The wood carver of "God the Father," which we have just seen, imitated the manner of Michelangelo but not his method. The solid, impressive beard of Moses became a delicate whirlwind of open forms in the beard of his friend God, as the wood carver made it.

Lincoln Memorial. Washington, D.C.

The Lincoln Memorial, in Washington, D. C., is an outstanding example of architecture, landscape design, and sculpture combined to form a monument to Abraham Lincoln, who is so revered by many Americans that he might almost be considered a god. The building even follows the plan of a Greek temple to house a seated statue, just as the temple at Olympia housed the enthroned king of the Greek gods.

Daniel Chester French, the American sculptor who created the figure of the President for the memorial, did not actually carve it. He made a model to be enlarged by professional stonecutters into the final statue three times life size, from several blocks of marble.

Lincoln occupies a thronelike bench, its two high sides ornamented with the Roman fasces, bundles of rods tied with bands, which symbolized authority. The vertical rods emphasize the great cube of the chair. The sculptor knew that as a geometric form a cube always suggests strength and steadfastness, two characteristics that are associated with Lincoln. He is seated in repose, his eyes gazing directly forward. One hand is open, relaxed, contemplative; the other is closed— a fist that suggests action. Obviously this statue is quite unlike Michelangelo's "Moses"—also a seated figure, but agitated, twisting, about to rise from his chair.

Lincoln, by Daniel Chester French. Lincoln Memorial.

Reproduced from the Collections of the Library of Congress

The Lincoln Memorial. Washington, D.C.

National Park Service, U.S. Department of the Interior

A piece of sculpture must be properly lighted if we are to appreciate its form. Light from above, coming down at a sharp angle, creates a pattern of highlights and shadows that reveal form. If the angle of light is too low, the sculpture appears flat because both the raised and depressed areas of the modeling are lighted. There are no shadows.

By day, light pours through the doorway of the Lincoln Memorial and tends to flatten the forms of the statue. Look again at the photograph of the building at dusk, when floodlights in the ceiling are the only source of light. Even at a distance the figure is impressive. The spirit of Lincoln truly seems to be present in his shrine.

Mount Rushmore National Memorial. Black Hills, South Dakota.

Mount Rushmore National Memorial is one of the man-made wonders of the United States. During fourteen years, starting in 1927 and with some interruptions due to lack of funds, Gutzon Borglum, the sculptor, struggled with the problems of carving from a granite mountain the faces of the four American Presidents that gaze out from the Black Hills of South Dakota.

The sculptor studied art in Europe, but returned to the United States as soon as possible because he wanted to create sculpture inspired by events and accomplishments in his native land. Above all, he thought, in keeping with the vastness of the country the sculpture of America should be colossal, with the same bigness as its skyscrapers, its far-flung highways and railroads. While explaining his ideas, he talked to so

20

opp. page   **Mount Rushmore National Memorial, South Dakota, by Gutzon Borglum.**

National Park Service, U.S. Department of the Interior

many people so persuasively that he was selected to be the sculptor for "the Shrine of Democracy," as the monument is sometimes called.

In it, Washington, the leader of our nation at its founding, is appropriately placed in front. Just behind him is Jefferson, the champion of liberty and government by the people. To the right, alone, is Lincoln, the preserver of our national unity and the defender of freedom for all people. Theodore Roosevelt, in the center, represents the progressive spirit of the United States, which he demonstrated by his building of the Panama Canal as part of his program to obtain economic freedom for the country.

Borglum first made a small model of the memorial. The stone-blasters and carvers enlarged the measurements of the model as they worked on the mountain. Sometimes cracks in the granite forced them to change the position of a head. For example, Jefferson was started farther forward, but was moved back to avoid a crack through the nose. The artist was afraid that if the head were carved in the first position, Jefferson's nose might fall off after several centuries.

Originally the sculptor planned to finish each figure down to the waist. (As we see, Washington's shoulders, coat lapels, and left arm are roughly indicated.) But rock conditions and other factors prevented the sculptor from completing his plan —perhaps fortunately for us, because nothing distracts our eyes from the four faces, each looking in a different direction to create variety in the grouping of the heads.

Crowning a mountaintop six thousand feet high, and visible for sixty miles, the faces on Mount Rushmore are images of American ideals and accomplishments as well as gods of the mountains and abiding spirits of the land. As sculpture, the monument they comprise may lack unity and some of the other elements of excellent sculptural form. It certainly does not lack one of the most important elements in any art—the decisive and powerful idea with which the artist sets to work.

THE IMAGE OF FAME

Statues of Rameses the Great. Abu Simbel, Egypt.

Rameses II was a famous king of ancient Egypt who ruled for more than sixty years. To honor various gods and to honor himself, he commanded many monuments to be erected during his reign. Each structure bore his name as "the living god," according to Egyptian religious beliefs. One of his most gigantic projects was the enormous temple to Horus, the Sun God, cut from the cliffs bordering the Nile River at Abu Simbel. Starting in about 1250 B.C., thousands of workmen labored twenty years to build this temple, which consisted of twelve chambers extending two hundred feet into the rock. Nine statues of Rameses loomed in the semidarkness within. Because the king wanted to be sure that his image of fame was eternal, his portrait statue was repeated four times outside, as pictured on the opposite page. Except for one that crashed to the ground, these figures gazed directly east for three thousand years. From these three remaining figures we can learn much about Egyptian sculpture.

Notice that each head looks forward, neither to the right nor to the left. The king sits squarely on his throne, both of his heels drawn back to its base, one hand resting on each knee, his arms close to his body. Each figure is compact and massive, almost rigid. Like the "Moses," by Michelangelo, such forms in sculpture are "closed" forms. They suggest majesty and endurance. Even small statues carved in this manner, like those of the queens and children at the king's feet, communicate the same feelings.

24

opp. page   **Statues of Rameses the Great. Abu Simbel, Egypt.**

The Egyptian artists realized that if such massive shapes were left rough, their images would appear crude and unattractive. Therefore they smoothed the surfaces and carved the details of the eyes, ears, noses, mouths, kneecaps, and muscles of the legs most delicately. But in order to preserve the weighty forms of faces and bodies they were careful not to make these features too prominent. In other words, the sculptors maintained balance between form and surface, at the same time achieving contrast between two different things—strength and refinement.

Doubtless Rameses thought that the temple at Abu Simbel would remain in place forever. He did not know that in the twentieth century A.D. a dam would be built that would back up the waters of the Nile so high that the statues and temple would be completely covered. To prevent the disappearance of this famous monument, many nations of the world have contributed funds to pay for the task of cutting the temple carefully into huge blocks and moving it to higher ground. Someday the building will be reassembled and the statues of Rameses the Great will once again greet the rising sun. His image of fame will endure.

The Discobolus. Therme Museum, Rome, Italy.

The Temple of Zeus at Olympia stood in a sacred grove of trees ornamented with statues of the athletes who had won contests in the Olympic games that took place nearby. The "Discobolus," or "Discus Thrower," is a monument to an athlete whose name unfortunately is not known. Designed as an image of fame, this statue has become a symbol of the

opp. page   **The Discobolus by Myron. Therme Museum, Rome.**
Alinari-Art Reference Bureau

Greek ideal of manly physical perfection. Copies of the original by Myron of Eleutherae, a Greek sculptor of the fifth century B.C., were made in Roman times and may be seen in several museums.

The Greeks were the first to use white marble extensively for their sculpture. Unlike denser stones, marble is crystalline in structure, like sugar. Light flows through its surface, creating an effect similar to light falling on human skin. The combination of form and light suggests life. We can see that the sculptor carved from stone, because he preserved "stoniness" by carving crisply, but the light-transmitting quality of marble gives the statue an alertness and vivacity that we associate with living beings.

In this statue an impression of movement also suggests aliveness. Myron chose that moment in the throw of the discus when the athlete's arm has reached the uppermost position of the swing—that instant when the body is still, frozen, before the discus, hand, and arm descend in a hurling motion. This body position is the one that can best be caught in motionless stone.

You may be surprised to learn that while the artist carved the muscles with great care in a pose that seems natural, he actually distorted nature to impress us with the grace, strength, and noble character of the athlete. With the upper part of the body twisted so far around, it is not possible to throw the discus a great distance. Such is the power of art to transform nature, thereby creating an image that seems to be the very essence of life.

Winged Victory. Louvre Museum, Paris, France.

This world-renowned statue occupies the place of honor on the grand staircase of the Louvre Museum, in Paris. More than twice life size, the powerful and majestic woman's form once stood at Samothrace in the northeast corner of the Aegean Sea. A certain king named Demetrius ordered the statue carved as a monument to a naval victory of his in 306 B.C., during a sea war with Egypt.

In 1867 the figure was found with its head and arms missing. Perhaps you ask the question, "How do you know what this statue represented when it was complete, fresh from the sculptor's chisel?" The answer is to be found on old coins minted by Demetrius a few years after the "Victory" was finished. They show the monument as a winged woman alighting on the prow of a ship, a trumpet to her lips, sounding forth the triumph of the king to the entire world. This statue was actually an image of fame, for this is the way that fame has been represented from ancient times to the present day, not only in sculpture, but in paintings and prints as well.

Greek sculptors sought to present forms in art that were ideal, perfect, as we have seen in the "Discus Thrower." The completely developed and balanced human form, often unclothed, expressed this perfection. When the figures were draped, as in the "Victory," the basic forms of the body were not hidden. Notice that the form of the left leg is visible through the very thin cloth that covers it. This revelation of form underneath overlaying fabric is one of the great accomplishments of Greek art. The "Three Fates" from the Parthenon, Athens—now in the British Museum, London—displays this same mastery. The "Winged Victory" 's rhythmical,

fluttering folds of drapery suggest movement and the rush of wind at sea. They also contrast by their delicacy with the grandeur of the woman's form and the horizontal sweep of her splendid wings.

Emperor Augustus. Vatican Museum, Rome, Italy.

Caesar Augustus, great-nephew of the famous Julius Caesar, was the first emperor of Rome. During his lifetime he strengthened the empire's defenses, won back certain territories seized by enemies, and established a lasting peace. We know from the images represented on the magnificent armor of this famous portrait-statue that it was completed after the emperor's successful campaigns, about 13 B.C.

The two central figures reenact an event of his eastern campaign when standards, similar to flags, which had been captured from the Roman army years before, were returned to Augustus. Other figures symbolize the provinces of Spain and Gaul. They are interspersed with gods and goddesses of the dawn, the sun, and the earth. These details, modeled in relief sculpture, may possibly have been copied from an actual breastplate made for the emperor by a sculptor who was also a metalworker, as most sculptors were in classical times. There is no doubt that the splendid corselet creates an impression of luxury and elegance most appropriate to the ruler of the Roman Empire.

Let us now consider other parts of the figure from the standpoint of sculpture in the round. The face does not have the smooth brow, straight nose, and full lips favored as "ideal" by the Greeks. The eyes and mouth are small, the nose larger

opp. page   **The Winged Victory. Louvre Museum, Paris.**

Archives Photographiques, Paris

in proportion to the face, because the sculptor had looked carefully at the emperor's features and blended them with the ideal features of Greek sculpture. He was trying to create a portrait and at the same time retain the impression of Greek art. Later Roman portrait sculpture was even more realistic, sometimes showing every wart and wrinkle.

At the foot of the statue, the small cupid riding on a dolphin is a symbol of the goddess Venus, from whom Augustus was supposed to have been descended.

Colleoni Monument. Campo San Zanipolo, Venice, Italy.

In Italy, during the artistic and literary period known as the Renaissance, a sculptor-goldsmith by the name of Andrea del Verrocchio received an order from the city of Venice to create a monument to General Bartolommeo Colleoni, a noted leader of the Venetian state. The artist worked on the memorial for a long time and had just completed a model of it before his death. Another sculptor supervised the casting of the model into bronze.

Bronze is a metal obtained by melting together copper and tin. The Greeks and Romans used this metal for making weapons, armor, household utensils, and statues. Very few bronze statues have survived from classical times because they were melted down for other uses. The most famous Greek bronze horses to escape the melting pot are those on the front of St. Mark's Cathedral, in Venice. They undoubtedly inspired Verrocchio to create one of the finest horse-and-rider monuments in the world.

Colleoni sits upright in his saddle, his legs straight, almost

33

opp. page   **The Emperor Augustus. Vatican Museum, Rome.**

Alinari-Art Reference Bureau

as if he were standing to his full height in the stirrups. His right hand draws back his general's baton. His left elbow thrusts forward as his body twists slightly one way and his head the other. We have seen a similar pose in Michelangelo's "Moses" and have noted how it expresses vitality, animation, and movement.

The sculptor allowed for the fact that the very high pedestal places the general's head quite far from us. He therefore modeled the face and helmet very sharply and clearly and exaggerated them somewhat, so that they still appear powerful and precise even when seen from a distance.

The head of General Colleoni's horse reveals the splendid possibilities of bronze for duplicating the most exact modeling of fine details, such as the veins, the folds of skin, the softly curling mane, and the elegant harness. These different textures were modeled and carved in a thin coating of beeswax that covered the entire heat-proof clay model of the horse and rider. When every detail was finished, the model was ready for casting in bronze by the procedure known as "the lost-wax process."

Essentially this method of casting requires the sculptor to cover the wax surface with a layer of heat-proof clay painted in liquid form on the wax to fill every crevice. When the clay has dried, more is added to make an outer mold through which small pipes are inserted down to the layer of wax. The model and the mold are then heated to melt the wax so that it is "lost" by running out of the tubes. This leaves a space to be filled by the melted bronze, which flows into every nook and cranny originally sculptured on the wax surface of the model.

The final statue was a bronze shell made thicker on the

35

inside in some places so that the extra weight would counter-balance the sculpture. It was thereby possible to pose the horse standing on three feet with one foot raised. Counter-balancing removed the possibility of the horse and rider toppling over as lead soldiers sometimes do.

Look at the picture of the entire monument and notice how the statue is placed on the pedestal. The body of the general is to the right of the central column of the base. Therefore the head and forefoot of the horse extend beyond the edge, out into the space that seems to flow past the statue, marvelously suggesting that the horse and rider are moving.

Voltaire. Louvre Museum, Paris, France.

François Arouet, known as Voltaire, was a noted French author of the eighteenth century. He sometimes criticized people and made fun of them in his writings, so annoying the king that he banished Voltaire from Paris on several occasions. These enforced leaves gave the author opportunity to visit other countries, where he was welcomed as a celebrity.

Jean Antoine Houdon, also a native of France, created a life-sized portrait statue of Voltaire — a monument to his fame. Several marble copies of the original clay model made by the sculptor exist. Other works by Houdon include a statue of George Washington in the State Capitol at Richmond, Virginia, and portraits of Benjamin Franklin and Thomas Jefferson.

Voltaire, like most people of his era, admired the ancients, especially the Romans. Houdon represented him as a Roman elder seated sedately in an elegant chair ornamented with

opp. page   **Colleoni Monument. Detail of horse's head.**

Alinari-Art Reference Bureau

VOLTAIRE.

finely chiseled leaves and grooves. The long, simple robe is like a Roman toga. The band around his head is like the Roman fillet, which was a mark of honor. The modeling of the robe and chair is simple and grand in the manner known as "ideal," inspired by classical sculpture. Now examine carefully the face and hand. They are not ideal, but detailed and natural. Voltaire looks to his right with an alert, mischievous expression. We can see tiny wrinkles of skin on his hand. Houdon might have been tempted to model the hair in the same exact way, but he realized that if the hair were elaborate it would draw our attention away from the face.

The sculptor once said, "It should be our aim to preserve and render imperishable the true form and image of the men who have brought honor and glory to their country." His skill at combining the ideal and the real achieved this aim, and he became one of the greatest portrait sculptors of all time.

Monument to Cézanne. Tuileries Garden, Paris, France.

Paul Cézanne was a leading French painter of the early twentieth century. He was dissatisfied with the methods used by other artists of his day and experimented with his own kind of painting. From nature, he selected forms that were geometrical, and arranged them according to principles of geometry. The cube, the cone, and the sphere inspired his admiration because they were stable and therefore grand and eternal.

While Cézanne was achieving success in his work another French artist, Aristide Maillol, experimented with ideas similar to Cézanne's, but in the field of sculpture. He devoted him-

39

opp. page   **Voltaire, by Houdon. Louvre Museum, Paris.**

Archives Photographiques, Paris

self almost exclusively to creating images of the unclothed female form. When Cézanne died, Maillol was asked to design a monument to the painter.

A memorial in the form of a reclining woman holding a laurel spray appealed to Maillol. Just as Cézanne admired paintings by old masters, so Maillol admired the sculpture of the Greeks and Romans, who often sculptured reclining figures, both clothed and unclothed. Laurel leaves as signs of honor or victory are also found in classical art.

The sculptor modeled the figure in clay, to be cast in lead. He kept the forms as simple as possible. The parts of the body are smoothly rounded and lifelike and at the same time they suggest geometric forms. To achieve sculptural variety he modeled the drapery very flatly, in contrast to the rounded forms. He also varied the folds of cloth. Some are sweeping curves; others are sharp, jagged angles.

Notice how the figure is stretched out in a long, curved line. The edge of the cloth under the body repeats this line.

Because the artist arranged the figure so skillfully, we hardly realize that the pose—leaning far backward and supported only on one elbow—is a rather awkward one for a human being to assume. Maillol had the ability to create from nature new images for our eyes to perceive—images that we must study carefully, that we may not accept at first. But when we do accept them, they become a part of our lives and our ways of seeing.

41

opp. page   **Monument to Cézanne, by Maillol. Tuileries Garden, Paris.**
Photographie Giraudon

Nelson's Column. Trafalgar Square, London, England.

On October 21, 1805, Lord Nelson, commander of the English fleet, engaged the ships of France and Spain off Cape Trafalgar on the Spanish coast. The English won, but their commander was killed during the battle. In 1829, plans were completed to erect a monument to honor Nelson in a newly designed London square bearing the battle's name. This square became the meeting place for all England.

A granite column rises to the height of 185 feet, surmounted by a bronze Corinthian capital and the statue of Nelson, over 17 feet high, by E. H. Baily. Four huge lions, designed by the noted animal painter Sir Edwin Landseer, guard the base. Four bronze reliefs on the pedestal depict Nelson's most important naval victories. Undoubtedly the column's designer, William Railton, remembered Roman triumphal columns like the Emperor Trajan's, but decided on the four reliefs rather than a spiraling scroll of sculpture from top to bottom.

The Nelson Column is a notable example of collaboration in the arts, as was the Lincoln Memorial in Washington. No single artist created it. Individually its sculptural elements are not remarkable. Collectively they form one of the most successful monuments in the world. The details, rich as they are in chiseled granite and bronze, are unimportant, especially at sunset when the sea lord atop his column, removed but ever present in the evening sky, becomes a symbolic shape with cocked hat and sword. Then we realize how important to sculpture is its outline or silhouette.

42

opp. page   Nelson's Column. Trafalgar Square, London.
The British Travel Association
Trajan's Column. The Forum, Rome.   *Alinari-Art Reference Bureau*

THE IMAGE OF COURAGE AND SACRIFICE

Relief from the Tomb of Emperor T'ai Tsung.
University Museum, Philadelphia, Pennsylvania.

In A. D. 637, the Emperor of China ordered his tomb to be erected outside his capital, at that time one of the most magnificent cities in the world. He had spent many years struggling with rebellious chieftains of several provinces, and forming their peoples and territories into a nation. He named his capital "The City of Everlasting Peace," to mark the end of wars, and so it remained for the period of over a hundred years known as the T'ang dynasty. This was a flourishing period for all the arts, but especially for the art of sculpture.

The Emperor was fond of the plucky horses that had carried him through his successful campaigns. To honor them, he ordered a room at the entrance to his mausoleum, with portraits of six of his favorite battle chargers. Two of these masterpieces of Chinese sculpture are now in the University Museum in Philadelphia. Autumn Dew, whose picture is on page 45, carried the Emperor during his conquest of Honan Province.

The horse stands stiff and immovable while a soldier pulls an arrow from his chest. Notice how the horse and the man almost completely fill the frame, thereby creating a very large and powerful image. The pattern of shapes is raised sharply from the background, but the forms are kept flat and parallel with it—a most appropriate sculptural treatment for a wall panel.

44   Beautiful lines represent the halter, saddle, and soldier's quiver of arrows clearly but not too prominently, because the

opp. page   **Relief from Tomb of Emperor T'ai Tsung.**

The University Museum of the University of Pennsylvania

great horse is the main subject of this monument. Trace the outline of the horse with your finger, starting at the top of his head. You will find it is one continuous wavering boundary to the shapes within it—not a series of crude, straight lines. Such splendid drawing may have come from the hand of the great artist of the period, Yen Li-pen.

Perhaps you are familiar with other horses of the T'ang period, made of baked clay and brilliantly colored. There are quite a few of these long-legged, lively animals decorated with elaborate harnesses. They were the show horses of the nobility and do not have the dignity or calm sturdiness of T'ai Tsung's battle chargers. The portrait of Autumn Dew was part of a memorial to the deeds of his master, but it was also a citation of bravery for the animal—a record of courage. As a tribute to an individual horse it is also a recognition of the nobility and faithfulness of all horses.

Lion of Lucerne. Lucerne, Switzerland.

One of the most photographed monuments in the world is hidden away in a rocky glen in Lucerne, Switzerland. A mighty lion, three times life size, lies mortally wounded, his right paw protecting the shield of France. Nearby is the shield of Switzerland. Above the cave sheltering the lion, large letters carved in the rock proclaim in Latin, "To the Loyalty and Bravery of the Swiss."

The Swiss to whom the inscription refers were members of the Swiss Guard hired by the King and Queen of France to protect them in their palace in Paris. When the mob stormed the palace to capture the monarchs during the French Revolution in 1792, the Swiss were faithful and re-

46

opp. page   The Lion of Lucerne, by Thorvaldsen. Lucerne, Switzerland.

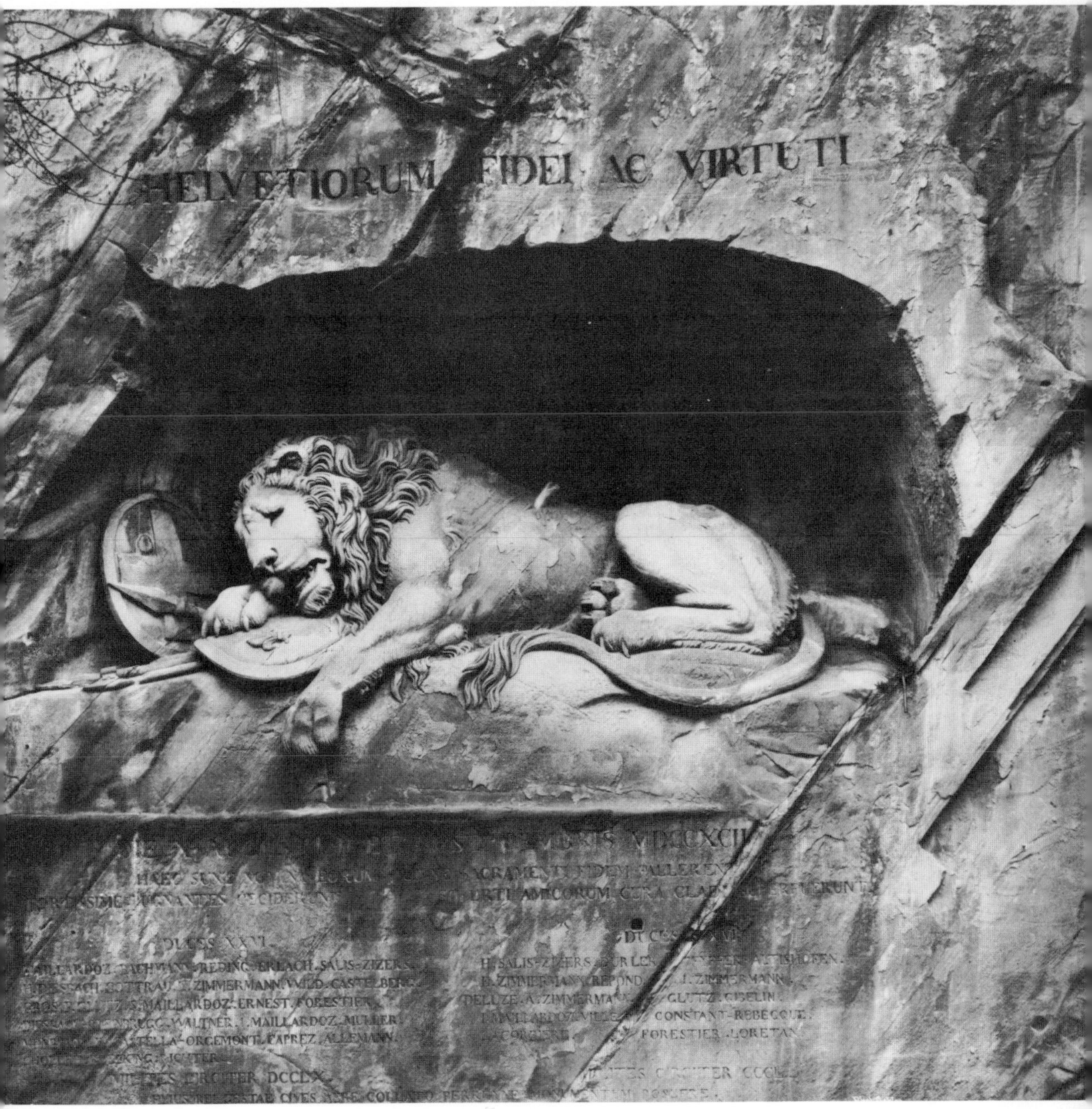
HELVETIORUM FIDEI AC VIRTUTI

mained at their posts. Many suffered death at the hands of the people. Years later, one of the former members of the Guard suggested that a memorial be created to honor his comrades' bravery and sacrifice. Bertel Thorvaldsen, the noted Danish sculptor, received the order to design the monument.

Thorvaldsen spent much of his life in Rome. He enthusiastically admired Greek and Roman sculpture. While he did not actually copy works by the ancients, he followed them so closely in his ideas and methods that his work is called neoclassical, meaning "new classical." When he modeled the great lion he departed somewhat from his usual style and achieved one of his best works — an image that is more natural than classical.

His clay model was cast in plaster and used by a stone carver as a guide for the final cutting into the rock. The sculptor must have studied the face of the cliff before he completed his model. We can see very clearly the layers of stone slanting from upper right to lower left to create a strong diagonal pattern. Thorvaldsen fitted the arrangement of the lion's body into this pattern so that the angle of the head is the same as the angle of the stone. The left leg and paw are also parallel to the seams of the rock.

The lion's body is very compact, following the principle of fine sculpture to be self-contained. Notice that what would have been an awkward space below the animal's body is filled in by the sinuous curve of the lion's tail. The sculptor considered carefully the effect of light on his work. As seen **48** against the mysterious black depth of the cave, the lion is placed so that the most important part of the body, the head, receives the most light. Such strong contrast of light and dark makes the memorial dramatic and tends to distract us from noticing that the body of the animal is not very strongly modeled. The lion's mane and tail reveal Thorvaldsen's love of classical sculpture, for they seem overly elaborate and too carefully arranged, in a way that we sometimes see in Roman statues.

Departure of the Volunteers. Arc de Triomphe, Paris, France.

The Arch of Triumph is a famous Paris landmark commemorating victories of the French army. Begun in 1806, it was not completed for thirty years. Several architects and sculptors worked on the monument. Among them was François Rude, who created the enormous high relief on the right side of the arch.

There are two centers of interest in this sculpture: the magnificently carved face of the Goddess of War, who is shouting her battle cry, and the face of the bearded man, who personifies leadership. A young boy looks up at the man with admiration. Four other men of different ages complete the group, with many details of weapons, shields, and even a horse's head.

Rude modeled the bodies carefully to emphasize their strong muscles. Each figure is posed differently, with arms and legs overlapping. This somewhat complicated arrangement suggests that there are more figures than actually appear—that this is an entire army vigorously marching.

As you see, Rude not only presented skillfully arranged forms, but he also paid close attention to the modeling of different textures. The rough chain-mail armor contrasts

49

Arc de Triomphe, Paris.   *Archives Photographiques, Paris*

50

opp. page   **Departure of the Volunteers, by Rude. Arc de Triomphe, Paris.**

Archives Photographiques, Paris

with the smooth muscles and skin. The costume of the goddess consists of flowing drapery and a short blouse of metal plates. She is carried on sweeping wings, many-feathered and powerful. Notice the straight line from the tip of her sword through her arm, her shoulder, and across her body to the sword's scabbard, flung out horizontally by the speed of her motion. This line emphasizes the rush of movement from right to left. Like the stirring music of the French national anthem, the overpowering image of the war goddess is sometimes called "The Marseillaise."

Burghers of Calais. Houses of Parliament Garden, London, England.

The fame of Auguste Rodin, the French sculptor, is almost as great as that of Michelangelo. Rodin lived from 1840 to 1917. His art looked backward—especially to the sculpture of the Middle Ages that he admired so much—and forward to the art of the twentieth century, which he helped to form. Although many of his works were carved in marble, he modeled his finest sculpture in clay to be cast into bronze. "The Burghers of Calais" is the largest and most elaborate of all his completed projects. Several castings of this group exist, all from the same mold. We shall look at the one set up in the gardens behind the Houses of Parliament in London.

In 1884 the city government of Calais, France, asked Rodin to create a monument to recall an important event that occurred in 1347. After almost a year of siege by the English king, Edward III, a small group of leading citizens decided to sacrifice themselves to save the other people of

53

opp. page   **Departure of the Volunteers, by Rude. Detail of head.**

Archives Photographiques, Paris

The Burghers of Calais, by Rodin. Houses of Parliament Garden, London.

Roger-Viollet

54

opp. page   **The Burghers of Calais, by Rodin. Detail of key bearer.**

Roger-Viollet

Calais. Taking the key to the city to give to the king, they marched out the gate, each clothed in rags of sackcloth woven of goat's hair, a symbol of repentance. They also wore rope halters to signify their willingness to be hanged. Straight to the king they went, and gave themselves up. The siege was lifted and the city saved.

This story of the Middle Ages appealed to Rodin. It was dramatic, heroic, and pathetic. He worked for several years, constantly changing the positions of the figures, which he modeled individually and then grouped in various ways. Finally he decided upon a very compact arrangement to signify that the men were all bound together by their spirit of sacrifice.

The men are about to leave the city. One has started to walk, his head inclined to the right, his body expressing determination and resignation. The second, a young man, turns back, as if saying, "Let us go!" We see the elbow of a third man whose hand is over his eyes as if to blot out the sight of what is to come. The old man in the center starts walking also, appearing to be lost in his thoughts. The key bearer stands bravely in the corner nearest us. Behind him is the only man in the group who has not fully made up his mind to follow. He turns away, his hands to his head in desperation.

The front view of the key bearer reveals Rodin's ability to show us form even in deep shadow. If you look closely you will see the key bearer's left eye deep in its cavernous socket. Notice also how sharply ridged are the folds of his mantle and how they fall, not straight down but from left to right, one after **56** another, in parallel lines that suggest that the body's movement is about to begin as he steps forward.

Rodin applied the clay to his figures in lumps and ridges, or he scooped out holes with his fingers in order to obtain as much variety of light and shadow as possible. Look for a moment at the hand of the man leading the others, reproduced as the frontispiece of this book. The sculptor's violent modeling of this hand reveals the bones, the flesh, and the skin with lights and darks as dramatic as if they had been painted on a canvas. No other sculptor pushed the art of sculpture so close to painting as did Rodin with the "color" he obtained through the play of light and shadow on his surfaces.

When people first saw the roughness of Rodin's sculpture they were shocked, because they were accustomed to nice, smoothly finished statues. They did not realize that the artist was expressing his ideas not only in the poses of his figures, the masses that form their bodies, but also in their surfaces —extremely rough for strong, bold ideas, less so for gentle ideas, but always with an infinite variation of shapes curving out to catch the light or curving in to hold the shadow. "The Burghers of Calais" is a fine example of sculpture strong in treatment, to express a grand and tragic image.

Navy-Merchant Marine Memorial. Washington, D.C.

In 1934, Gaston Lachaise completed this memorial to Americans lost at sea—a great wave in bronze, surmounted by flying gulls, that stands on Columbia Island in the Potomac River near Washington, D. C. Unfortunately, few visitors to the nation's capital see this monument because it is almost completely hidden by the trees along the boulevard to Mount Vernon.

Lachaise was born in France but made his home in the United States, where he achieved fame for his large bronze statues of women with greatly exaggerated arms and legs, standing on tiny, pointed feet. All his sculpture reveals his preference for swelling forms seemingly bursting with life from within, but poised delicately, in balance.

As we look at his image of the breaking wave we sense the curving, powerful surge of the sea. The curling edge of water is about to cover the winged shield honoring those men of the Navy and Merchant Marine who "have given life or still offer it in the performance of heroic deeds." On either side of the shield the sculptor placed the insignia of the two services, modeling them in beautiful low relief on plaques suggesting the backs of horseshoe crabs ornamented with shells and trailing, elegant scrolls like the tentacles of octopuses. Here and there in the crevices of the leaflike forms of spray hundreds of tiny seeds and the eggs of sea creatures cling. The wave is therefore an image of the oceans of the world, teeming with the power of life.

In contrast to the motion of the wave to the right, the flight of birds above it moves to the left. This creates the delicate stability that Lachaise sought in all his sculpture. The gulls' bodies are rounded, supported on strong wings, their feathers repeating the flat ridges of the wave. Balance and rhythm—two important controlling devices found in all the arts—are very evident in this handsome monument.

opp. page　　**Navy-Merchant Marine Memorial, by Lachaise. Washington, D.C.**
Robert W. Lishman

Trade Union War Memorial. Congress House, London, England.

Jacob Epstein, an American, studied sculpture in Paris, where he admired the works of Rodin. He then went to live in England and soon became famous for his portraits of noted people. These were done in bronze, and his technique of surfacing the material with innumerable ridges, furrows, and small particles to catch light and create shadow was based on Rodin's method. He was also careful to show the structure beneath the surface.

There are a few sculptural pieces that Epstein carved out of stone. The "Trade Union War Memorial" is a fine example of this phase of his work. A massive figure carrying the limp but compact form of a fallen soldier strides toward us. The long, smooth robe worn by the figure is like a background curtain to set off the hands holding the soldier's body and the forms of the body itself, with the muscular arm and legs hanging absolutely straight. Notice that the face of the figure looks directly ahead; the eyes are large; the mouth and jaw thrust forward almost defiantly. We are reminded of the majesty and simplicity of Egyptian sculpture and of African idols and other sculpture of tribal origin.

The sculptor knew the great art of the past, including the theme of the "Pieta," the Mother of Christ holding her dead son, of which this statue seems a recollection. As a follower of Rodin, who believed that the sculptor creates images from nature but stresses and emphasizes whatever forms he wishes, Epstein achieved sculpture that upon first acquaintance seems brutal and ugly. By following his own conscience and artistic beliefs he helped to free sculpture from a tradition of "pretti-

60

opp. page   **Trade Union War Memorial, by Epstein. Congress House, London.**
News Division, British Information Services

ness." He also helped to establish the modern view that each work of art must be looked at for its own sake—not as a copy of nature, but for the image that it presents.

This Is the Place Monument. Salt Lake City, Utah.

Brigham Young, leader of the Church of Jesus Christ of Latter-day Saints, departed in 1847 from Council Bluffs, Iowa, with his followers, known as Mormons. They traveled on horseback and in wagons over a trail leading westward, to find a homeland, a place where they could establish their own community and church without fear of religious hatred or persecution.

After four months of toilsome travel over a road they sometimes made themselves through the wilderness, they arrived within sight of Great Salt Lake. Scouts sent ahead returned to say that they thought they had found the right place to settle. When the wagon bearing Brigham Young, ill with mountain fever, stopped at the top of Big Mountain Pass, he looked at the expanse of lake and land below and said, "It is enough. This is the right place. Drive on." One hundred years later, a few miles below the spot, a monument was dedicated to commemorate the arrival of the Mormons at the end of their trail. It also pays honor to other explorers who journeyed in the West.

Mahonri Young, grandson of Brigham Young, was asked to create the sculpture for this structure. It is actually a building containing a large mural painting depicting events on the Mormons' march. Young studied his art with the American sculptors Saint-Gaudens and Daniel Chester French and with

62

opp. page   **This is the Place Monument, by Young. Salt Lake City, Utah.**

Church Information Service The Church of Jesus Christ of

Latter-Day Saints

various teachers in Paris. He was familiar with many of the famous monuments of the world before he began this sculptured tribute to his forebears.

Three figures dominate the monument because of their position atop the central pylon and because they are sculptured twice life size. Brigham Young stands in the center, his trusted companions, Heber C. Kimball and Wilford Woodruff, on either side. At the foot of the pylon are the two scouts who reported joyously that they had sighted a likely place. The rhythm of movement of this group is excellent. Notice how the upraised hands holding their hats contrast with the arching neck of the horse reaching down to graze.

The explorer groups at either end of the building are also skillfully arranged, with the central figure of each raised up on his horse to create a focal point. A low relief in bronze, depicting the wagon train, connects the ends to the center, thereby unifying the parts into one harmonious whole. Notice that the sculptor did not subordinate his sculpture to the architecture nor did he smother the monument with sculptural details. He maintained a balance.

This monument is a good example of collaboration between an architect and a sculptor. They realized that unless their project loomed large against its mountain background, the work of man would appear insignificant compared with the work of nature. Therefore they established the height at sixty feet and the length at eighty-six feet to create one of the largest monuments in the United States.

64

THE IMAGE OF LIBERTY

Liberty Enlightening the World. New York Harbor, New York.

History tells us many tales of courage and sacrifice for the cause of liberty. It is surprising that there are not more sculptured images of this cherished hope of all people who are not free. Perhaps the Statue of Liberty has become so famous throughout the world that no other image of this idea is possible.

"Miss Liberty," as she is often called, has stood at the entrance to New York Harbor since 1886. The Alsatian sculptor Frédéric Auguste Bartholdi created her as a gift from the people of France to the United States, to commemorate the friendship between the two countries that began on July 4, 1776—the date inscribed on the tablet in her left hand. In her right hand she holds aloft a torch, its rays, like the rays of her crown, sending the light of freedom to all corners of the earth. A broken chain and shackle at her feet symbolize her power to break the bonds of tyranny and oppression.

In 1881, Bartholdi asked his friend Alexandre Gustave Eiffel, designer of the Eiffel Tower in Paris, to plan a steel framework for the statue, which was erected in New York. Meanwhile, Bartholdi and his assistants prepared wooden molds following the sculptor's design. Sheets of copper were shaped by hammering them over the molds. These copper forms were shipped to the United States for assembly on the steel framework. The noted American architect Richard M. Hunt planned the pedestal. Thus was created a colossal statue rising to the height of 305 feet.

The practical consideration of stability in all kinds of weather may have influenced Bartholdi to shape the body as a tall, thick column with a broad base and rather flat folds of drapery over which the wind could pass easily. The sculptural forms therefore seem somewhat weak, echoing but not achieving the grandeur of classical sculpture. Fortunately the idea of the Statue of Liberty was so clear and majestic in the sculptor's mind that he was able to create a noble image in spite of the deficiencies in sculptural form.

THE IMAGE OF DEATH

Monument to Hegeseo. National Museum, Athens, Greece.

Outside the gates of the cities of ancient Greece there was a "Street of Tombs" where memorial tablets were erected. It was customary to represent the dead persons as engaged in occupations they pursued during their lifetime. On page 68 we see one of the finest of these marble reliefs—a monument to Hegeseo, daughter of Proxenos of Athens. Her name is carved on the lintel of the doorway and she is seated on a graceful chair and attended by a serving maid who holds a jewel box. Possibly Hegeseo is selecting a large pin with which to fasten her robe.

How did the sculptor achieve this masterpiece? The forms of the two women fill the rectangle, but they do not crowd it. There is ample space between their heads and under the chair. In contrast to the space suggested by the flat background, the figures are carved in rounded relief. Notice how clearly the faces are modeled. The marble was carved away

67

opp. page   Statue of Liberty, by Bartholdi. New York Harbor.

behind the features to edge them with a dark line of shadow. In real life, the faces, being farther from the viewer, would appear less clear than the objects in the foreground—the legs of the chair and the lady's foot. To balance the top and bottom of a relief, most Greek sculptors emphasized the head. In this case, the balance also strengthens the image of a noble woman, serene in life as she was in death. This is a happy scene. It reminds us of the words of the poet Goethe, who wrote, "No people of the earth has so sweetly dreamed the dream of life as the Greeks."

Etruscan Sarcophagus. Louvre Museum, Paris, France.

Northwest of Rome, Italy, there once lived a nation of mysterious people known to the Romans as the Etruscans. They flourished for several centuries in a period before the Christian era, and through commerce with the Greeks, learned Greek customs, music, and poetry. The handsome sarcophagus illustrated on page 70 was modeled for an Etruscan nobleman and is now in the Louvre Museum, in Paris.

A smiling, bearded man, bare to the waist and with broad shoulders, reclines on a banqueting couch, one arm across his wife's shoulder, the other resting on a cushion. His wife, smiling also, wears a hat. Her hair hangs in braids on either side of her throat with its high collar. It is likely that the man held a wine cup, and his wife a mirror, for the Etruscans believed that if one carried a mirror to the Underworld after death, the soul contained in the mirror would not become separated from the body, provided that the mirror was carefully guarded.

69

opp. page   **Monument to Hegeseo. National Museum, Athens.**

Athens National Museum

Etruscan Sarchophagus. Louvre Museum, Paris. *Archives Photographiques, Paris*

opp. page   **Etruscan Sarcophagus. Detail.**   *Archives Photographiques, Paris*

This piece of sculpture is actually a covered coffin formed by the couch and mattress to contain the remains of the dead person. Made entirely of red clay that was modeled when moist and soft and then hardened by baking in an oven, the sarcophagus was also painted with designs on the couch rails, and the faces and robes were touched with color to make them appear more lifelike.

A close look at the two figures as seen from the corner of the couch reveals the way they were modeled according to the principles of fine sculpture. The forms of the bodies and heads are large, and rounded into simple shapes. They seem solid, with space flowing around them. In contrast to the large forms, the details of eyes, noses, mouths, ears, hair, and folds of drapery are very simply modeled. They decorate the large forms with restraint and thereby do not detract from them. (The hands are restorations, so we cannot judge them as Etruscan modeling.)

The image of death in this sculpture is really an image of the cheerful and luxurious life of the Etruscans and shows us clearly that they enjoyed feasting, wine, and music. The two smiling, alert faces could well be those of people listening to the sound of the flute, one of the Etruscans' favorite instruments.

Tomb of a Knight Templar. Temple Church, London, England.

Sculpture flourished in England during the Middle Ages, especially as decoration for churches and cathedrals. During the religious wars, vandals pulled down many statues from their places on church fronts, but spared the tombs of noted

opp. page   **Tomb of Knight Templar. Temple Church, London.**

Marburg-Art Reference Bureau

persons. Many of these were damaged by bombs in 1941, however. Among those damaged was the effigy pictured on page 73—one of nine in Temple Church, London. Fortunately, before the war, casts of the figures were made for the Victoria and Albert Museum. These casts served as models in restoring the damaged monuments.

The Knights Templars were members of a religious-military order established by the Crusaders to protect pilgrims and the Holy Sepulcher in Jerusalem. This tomb was carved about A. D. 1250, shortly after the English Knights Templars built their own church in London.

"Effigy" is another word for "likeness." The purpose of an effigy was to represent as closely as possible the features of a person at the time of death. Sometimes plaster molds were made over the face and used by the sculptor to obtain a true likeness—an image of death that was matter-of-fact, straightforward, and simple.

The unknown sculptor who created this figure (sometimes thought to represent Richard the Lion-Hearted) was a skillful artist. The man lies with one leg crossed over the other, in a position invented by sculptors at Wells Cathedral. This pose appears informal and natural, as if the knight had fallen from his horse, his sword under him, and his shield drawn partially over him as his hands were crossed in death. Notice the different textures represented in marble: the flexible chain mail, the shiny metal of shield and masklike helmet, the cloth tunic, and the ornamented leather belt.

Tomb of Medea Colleoni, by Amadeo. Colleoni Chapel, Bergamo. *Alinari-Art Reference Bureau*

Tomb of Medea Colleoni. Colleoni Chapel, Bergamo, Italy.

We have looked at one monument to a member of the Colleoni family, the great equestrian statue of the general, in Venice. He was buried at Bergamo, in a splendid chapel designed by the noted architect-sculptor Giovanni Antonio Amadeo, who had also created a beautiful tomb for the general's daughter some years before. This monument, pictured on page 75, is one of the masterpieces of Italian Renaissance sculpture, achieved during that wave of enthusiasm for the art and philosophy of the Greeks and Romans.

Medea lies on top of her sarcophagus. She wears a long robe of rich material, its design exquisitely indicated in very low relief. A collar of pearls encircles her long, slender neck. Her eyes are serenely closed, her long-fingered hands crossed one over the other. Above her a Latin inscription states her name, parentage, and the date of her death. Notice that the words are carved as if they had been lettered on a scroll of parchment. The lower right-hand corner of the scroll is beginning to curl.

In contrast to the natural, human form of the girl, represented realistically and ornamented in low relief, her sarcophagus is architectural, in classical form, enriched with high relief. Four pilasters divide the rectangle of the box into three sections and support the cornice at the top. Two panels contain shields bearing the insignia of her family, encircled with handsome wreaths of leaves and fruits bound with ribbons. In the center, a high relief depicts two angels attending Christ, who is pointing to the spear wound in His side. This scene echoes the art of the Middle Ages just before the

Renaissance, when religious sculpture was the primary task of most sculptors. The base of the sarcophagus is less elaborate than the cornice, in order not to detract from the heads of cherubim supporting the entire structure.

Amadeo completed Medea's tomb at a moment of perfect balance in Italian sculpture. Line and form are in equilibrium and so are relief sculpture and sculpture in the round. This image of death is not quite as matter-of-fact as the one we saw in the Knight Templar's tomb. Refinement and elegance enhance a simple theme. As we shall see presently, the images of Italian sculpture changed from the joyous calm of the Renaissance to the dramatic splendor of the period to follow, known as the Baroque.

Monument and Sarcophagus of Pope Urban VIII. St. Peter's Basilica, Rome, Italy.

Urban VIII, Pope from 1623 to 1644, employed the sculptor Giovanni Lorenzo Bernini, whose accomplishments and fame almost equaled those of Michelangelo, eighty years before. After the Pope's death, Bernini completed his tomb for St. Peter's Basilica, in Rome, one of the largest churches in the world. Because a small monument would have been lost in the vastness of the building, the sculptor erected an enormous piece of sculpture to serve as both monument and tomb. Unlike Amadeo, who used one material, white marble, for Medea Colleoni's sarcophagus, Bernini utilized several materials of different colors and textures to create an image of death as sumptuous as possible.

The bronze figure of the Pope sits enthroned, his hand

77

raised in blessing. The folds of his heavy robes zigzag across his body to create a feeling of power and energy. Below him the bronze skeleton of Death inscribes the papal name in gold on an open book. The wings of Death curve downward into the sarcophagus of dark marble, which is elaborately carved, and supported on lions' feet. On either side are allegorical figures that represent ideas. The woman on the right, bearing a sword, is Justice. The woman on the left, with a child in her arms, is Charity. Bernini included these two Virtues to indicate that Pope Urban was a just and charitable man.

If you look carefully to the left of the head of Justice you will see two very large bronze bees. They were placed there as a sign that Urban belonged to the noble family of the Barberini, identified for several centuries by the bee on their coat of arms.

This memorial is complicated, composed of many parts. It is very grand because the sculptor knew how to use his materials to advantage, especially to achieve dramatic contrasts of light and dark. He was also skillful with the voluminous draperies that clothe his figures and give them the majesty and agitation of the Baroque age.

War Memorial. Antoniter Church. Cologne, Germany.

We have just seen an Angel of Death, the somewhat gruesome skeleton on a Pope's tomb. The monument illustrated on page 80 is another Angel of Death by one of the great German sculptors of the twentieth century. This

opp. page   **Tomb of Pope Urban VIII, by Bernini.**

Alinari-Art Reference Bureau

memorial to the dead of two world wars is extremely simple and, in its way, as dramatic as the much more elaborate monument by Bernini.

Ernst Barlach lived at the same time as Cézanne and Maillol. Like them, he wished to create images close to geometric forms, reducing detail to a minimum, eliminating anything small or trivial. His Angel of Death has neither wings nor arms. Even the body is scarcely discernible under the heavy robe.

Notice how the line of the nose arches up into the eyebrows and circles around the very large closed eyes. The hair frames the face with the same curve. The slightly jagged neckline of the robe casts a deep shadow to emphasize the forward projection of the head. The angular lines of nostrils, mouth, and chopped-off hair contrast with the curves and strengthen the image. The overall line or direction of the figure is almost straight, sweeping from head to foot, varied slightly by the folds of the robe.

Most remarkably, the monument hangs in space, supported on twisted rods that blend in with the architecture so that they are almost invisible. The massive figure seems to float, almost to move. Space surrounds it and it pushes into space. This interaction between space and form becomes more noticeable in works by present-day sculptors. Barlach pointed the way for them in this greatly simplified abstracted image of death. For all its weight and boldness, this monument expresses something to be sensed through our feelings rather than through our minds. Without any symbols of war, a modern allegorical figure quietly and firmly speaks of courage, death, and peace.

81

opp. page   **War Memorial, by Barlach. Antoniter Church, Cologne.**
Rheinisches Bildarchiv

The Great Buddha of Kamakura. Kamakura, Japan.

Consulate General of Japan, N.Y.

THE IMAGE OF THE UNSEEN

Great Buddha of Kamakura. Kamakura, Japan.

The city of Kamakura was once the capital of Japan. More than a million people lived there and many of the inhabitants were believers in Buddhism, a form of religion founded by a prince of India, Gautama Buddha. The teachings of Buddha emphasize the importance of the unseen things that are eternal, rather than the visible things of the world that do not last. A person can approach the eternal through contemplation.

A colossal statue of Buddha was erected at Kamakura in A.D. 1252. It is over forty-two feet high and is the work of Japanese sculptors who were very skillful in the art of bronze-casting. The Buddha sits cross-legged with his hands on his lap, the palms turned upward and the thumbs touching. This is the hand position for contemplation established by the Buddhist religion—the symbolic indication of steady calm and faith in becoming one with the invisible.

The face of the Buddha is inclined toward us. In the center of his forehead is a round silver knob called the "urna," a mark that represents the wisdom of Buddha. His eyes, inlaid with gold, are veiled by lowered lids, shutting out the sights of the world.

The body of Buddha is modeled in simple, rounded forms that are a contrast to the rhythm of the delicate folds of his robe. In some sculpture, curving lines suggest movement. Here, because the lines are parallel, they suggest quiet life and harmony, and by their downward direction increase our impression of weighty repose and meditation.

The statue was originally enclosed in a wooden temple, which was swept away by a tidal wave. Another building was constructed, but in 1495 it too was destroyed. Meanwhile the population of Kamakura had moved away. Most of the buildings of the city disappeared, but the statue remained and the land around it became a beautiful park. A small temple was built to the right of the statue and there is a quiet chapel in the base of the figure. An opening in the folds of the robe allows a small amount of light to penetrate and shine on the altar.

Followers of Buddha believe that meditation requires deep concentration in order to shut out the sights and sounds and odors of the world around them. Truth cannot come unless a person separates himself completely from the physical world in order to be illuminated by the light of the spirit. It is, therefore, most appropriate that the Japanese name for the Buddha of Kamakura means the "Great Buddha of Infinite Light." Pause for a moment, concentrate your eyes on the entire figure, think only of this representation of Buddha. Perhaps you will experience a feeling of being slowly separated from the world around you. You will experience one of the objectives of art: to transport us out of ourselves—in this example of sculpture, to make us see an image of the unseen.

Adams Memorial. Rock Creek Cemetery, Washington, D.C.

Henry Adams was a famous American historian and writer. He lived in Washington, where his home was a meeting place for noted people of the world, including the American sculp-

opp. page   **The Adams Memorial, by Saint-Gaudens.**

Rock Creek Cemetery, Washington, D.C.

*Reproduced from the Collections
of the Library of Congress*

tor Augustus Saint-Gaudens and the American painter and stained-glass designer John La Farge. When Mrs. Adams died suddenly, her husband asked the two artists to plan a monument to his wife. La Farge was familiar with the oriental art of China and Japan. Saint-Gaudens had studied sculpture in Europe and knew the works of the Greeks and Romans. The monument, primarily the work of the sculptor, is one of the best-known examples of sculpture in the United States, even though it is not in a prominent place in the city, but hidden away in a grove of trees in Rock Creek Cemetery.

A bronze figure, heavily robed and larger than life, sits on a throne of rough stone with a large rock as a footstool. Behind the figure is a slab of smooth granite surmounted by a cornice ornamented with the famous egg-and-dart molding of antiquity. The same smooth granite forms an architectural base for the statue and a bench opposite for visitors. Seated there, one is placed by the sculptor at a definite viewing distance to look at the face of the figure—a solemn face with eyes closed, hidden in the depth of shadow cast by the hood over the forehead. The right hand seems to hold the hood slightly away, as if to prevent the cloth from falling so low that the face would be completely veiled. All other details of the figure are obscured, submerged in fold upon fold—large and strong forms in bronze, crisscrossed in tiny ridges to catch the light.

A number of different sensations arise as we look at this statue. We seem to be in the presence of a majestic power completely at peace. There is a suggestion of rude strength, of the far past in the time of the Druids. There is also refinement in the face and hand.

John La Farge wrote some notes, jotting down ideas concerning the memorial, to give to his friend Saint-Gaudens. He mentioned Nirvana, that state of non-being when the soul is merged with the divine, according to the beliefs of the followers of Buddha. If you look back to the "Great Buddha of Kamakura," you may see that there is an echo of the other-worldliness of oriental art in the "Adams Memorial."

King of Kings. Solomon R. Guggenheim Museum, New York.

Constantin Brancusi was born in Rumania. He loved the rocks and trees of his homeland in the Carpathian Mountains. Later he came to France, where he spent the rest of his life except for a journey to India. But he always remembered the forms of nature and represented them in his sculpture. He worked alone in his Paris studio and lived very quietly, inspired by the writings of a Tibetan poet-monk who preached the virtues of solitude and simplicity.

The Maharajah of Indore invited Brancusi to visit him in 1937 to discuss plans for a Temple of Deliverance. The sculptor returned to France and created "King of Kings." For many years this sculpture was entitled "Spirit of the Buddha," in keeping with its intended location as the central piece for a religious building in India. Unfortunately the temple was never built, and so the name of the statue was changed.

We must look at this sculpture as an image that expresses the very essence of an idea: in this case, an image of the spirit of Buddha rather than Buddha in human form, as we saw him at Kamakura, Japan. Brancusi selected wood as the

material for this image because he wanted to show us that, as a tree draws strength from the ground, so the spirit of Buddha is rooted in nature. The black ovals of the base suggest the depths of earth out of which life spirals through the conflicting desires of the body up to the mind. In contrast to the dark ovals of the base, the large, round eye sockets give forth the light of deliverance from the world of the flesh. The lotus flower, symbol of divine birth and immortality, crowns the head.

Now forget completely the above interpretation. Look at the tall, thin, closed form. If you had not been given an explanation of Brancusi's art, it is likely that you still would have received a similar impression of its purpose. Brancusi's image is powerful. It is close to us and at the same time far away. We are seen by the unseeing eyes of a spirit. If you look at this image long enough, you may begin to have a feeling of your own self freed from your body—the sensation of deliverance that the sculptor sought to achieve in all his works.

Memorial Figure. Dartington Hall, South Devon, England.

Henry Moore, famous sculptor of the twentieth century, has favored the image of the reclining figure throughout his long career. The "Memorial Figure," pictured on page 90, honors the memory of Christopher Martin, administrator of the Arts Center at Dartington Hall, England.

The photographs on page 92, taken at different stages during the carving of the figure show the sculptor's method of releasing his image from the block of stone. Unlike Michel-

89

angelo, who carved from the front view backward, Moore established the large forms first, by working around his block from all sides. Only three large forms compose this sculpture: the head and shoulders, the right leg, and the left leg. The forms are simple and bold, with flowing contours, and are connected by curving lines and grooves that suggest drapery covering the human shape. Moore was careful to preserve the "stoniness" of his material as he carved. He did not want the finished work to look as if it were stone transformed into flesh, but rather to suggest that stone had happened in the form of a woman.

When first seen, this compact sculpture creates the impression of calm repose. We are drawn to look at the figure from every side, to walk around it, to "feel" it, not with our hands, but with our eyes and minds. Gradually we realize that the forms are bursting with life, pushing out in space that flows into and around the figure. The shape of space is therefore as important as the shape of the figure itself. Moore has said, "A cave is a shape, not the mountain over it."

How does this figure become an image of the unseen? We must remember that it is a memorial to a person, just as Maillol's figure was a monument to Cézanne. Both sculptures go beyond their practical purposes, to become poetic symbols. Several people think that the sculpture of Henry Moore signifies the growing consciousness of the unity of mankind on earth. This figure is one of the first of the sculptor's presentations of this noble theme.

opp. page **Memorial Figure, by Henry Moore. Dartington Hall, England.**

Chaplin Jones

Bijenkorf Monument. Rotterdam, Netherlands.

The Russian-American sculptor, Naum Gabo, is the leading "Constructivist" sculptor in the world. His monument completed in the Netherlands in 1957 is his largest work. It rises to the height of eighty-five feet next to the Bijenkorf department store, designed by the architect Marcel Breuer, in central Rotterdam.

Most of the buildings in the city are new, because all the old ones were virtually destroyed by bombs in World War II. When the store directors invited Gabo to design a monument, he decided to keep in mind, as he worked on the project, the fortitude and persistence of the citizens of Rotterdam who had raised a new city so quickly after the war's end.

The image that Gabo created is not an image of fortitude and persistence. It is an image in itself, composed by the intelligence and skill of the artist—an image seen only in his mind's eye, unseen by everyone else until the sculptor made it visible.

What are the visual means that the artist uses to construct an image? Gabo has answered this question in his writings: (1) the lines of its contours; (2) the shapes enclosed by these lines; (3) the colors and textures of its surfaces; (4) the forms its volumes occupy in space. Let us look for these elements in the Bijenkorf Monument.

Eight ribs of steel (lines) rise to the sky. They define the contours and they also indicate rhythm by repetition (four outer and four inner ribs). They express forces, as well, because they are twisted like certain trees in the forest, which the sculptor had noted were stronger than their straight

93

companions. The inner form of bronze is a different color and texture from the steel ribs. All the forms are transparent, so that light and air flow unhindered through them. Space and form are interlocked in harmony.

The sculptor has given us a definition of the word "constructive." It implies much more than the fact that his sculpture is assembled. He has said, "Anything is constructive that enhances life, propels it, and adds something to it in the direction of growth, expansion, and development." Certainly this could be said not only of Gabo's sculpture, but of all sculpture, and indeed, of all the arts.

opp. page **The Bijenkorf Monument, by Gabo. Rotterdam, Netherlands.**
Courtesy of the artist

SCULPTORS REPRESENTED IN THIS BOOK

Giovanni Antonio Amadeo (1447?-1522)	Italian
Edward Hodges Baily (1788-1867)	English
Ernst Barlach (1870-1938)	German
Frédéric Auguste Bartholdi (1834-1904)	Alsatian
Giovanni Lorenzo Bernini (1598-1680)	Italian
Gutzon Borglum (1871-1941)	American
Constantin Brancusi (1876-1957)	Rumanian
Jacob Epstein (1880-1959)	American-English
Daniel Chester French (1850-1931)	American
Naum Gabo (1890-)	Russian-American
Jean Antoine Houdon (1741-1828)	French
Gaston Lachaise (1882-1935)	French-American
Aristide Maillol (1861-1944)	French
Master H. L. (Active, 1526)	German
Michelangelo Buonarrotti (1475-1564)	Italian
Henry Moore (1898-)	English
Myron of Eleutherae (Active, 450 B. C.)	Greek
Phidias (490?-432 B. C.)	Greek

Auguste Rodin (1840-1917)	French
François Rude (1784-1855)	French
Augustus Saint-Gaudens (1848-1907)	American
Bertel Thorvaldsen (1768-1844)	Danish
Andrea del Verrocchio (1435-1488)	Italian
Mahonri Mackintosh Young (1877-1957)	American

Unknown sculptors of:

Christ of Amiens	French
Emperor Augustus	Roman
Fertility God	Assyrian
Great Buddha	Japanese
Hegeseo Monument	Greek
Knight Templar Tomb	English
Rameses Statues	Egyptian
Sarcophagus	Etruscan
Shiva Trimurti	Indian
Sphinx	Egyptian
T'ai Tsung Relief	Chinese
Winged Victory	Greek

INDEX

99

The text of this book is composed in 12 point Optima Regular; the captions and titles in Optima Semi-Bold. Optima was designed by Hermann Zapf and cast at the Stempel Type Foundry, Frankfurt, Germany. This elegant modern typeface is increasingly used by modern designers for its clarity as well as its beauty.

☐ Designed by Joel Levy